W0114647

penguin life

climate

Whitney Hanson is the author of *home* and *harmony*. Through Whitney's vulnerability and authenticity, she has connected with thousands of readers, and she adamantly believes that poetry is not a dead language; rather it is the key to unlocking true vulnerability, which leads to deeper connection with one another. Whitney grew up in rural Montana and lives in Montana.

climate

whitney hanson

life

PENGUIN BOOKS
An imprint of Penguin Random House LLC
1745 Broadway, New York, NY 10019
penguinrandomhouse.com

Copyright © 2022, 2025 by Whitney Hanson
Penguin Random House values and supports copyright.
Copyright fuels creativity, encourages diverse voices, promotes
free speech, and creates a vibrant culture. Thank you for buying
an authorized edition of this book and for complying with
copyright laws by not reproducing, scanning, or distributing
any part of it in any form without permission. You are
supporting writers and allowing Penguin Random House to
continue to publish books for every reader. Please note that no
part of this book may be used or reproduced in any manner
for the purpose of training artificial intelligence
technologies or systems.

A Penguin Life Book

Set in Adobe Caslon Pro
Designed by Sabrina Bowers

LIBRARY OF CONGRESS CATALOGING-IN-PUBLICATION DATA
Names: Hanson, Whitney, author.
Title: Climate / Whitney Hanson.
Description: [First edition] | New York : Penguin Life, 2025.
Identifiers: LCCN 2024046940 (print) |
LCCN 2024046941 (ebook) | ISBN 9780593994238 (paperback) |
ISBN 9780593994245 (ebook)
Subjects: LCGFT: Poetry.
Classification: LCC PS3608.A72336 C55 2025 (print) |
LCC PS3608.A72336 (ebook) |
DDC 811/.6—dc23/eng/20241018
LC record available at https://lccn.loc.gov/2024046940
LC ebook record available at https://lccn.loc.gov/2024046941

First self-published in the United States of America 2022
Published with an introduction and additional poems in
Penguin Books 2025

Printed in the United States of America
1st Printing

The authorized representative in the EU for product safety and
compliance is Penguin Random House Ireland, Morrison
Chambers, 32 Nassau Street, Dublin D02 YH68, Ireland,
https://eu-contact.penguin.ie.

for those whose rainclouds
feel too heavy to shoulder

contents

introduction

When I first published *climate* I was in a season of shedding my skin. I was feeling the aftershocks of loss and learning that change is both inevitable and deeply uncomfortable. Writing this book was a process of excavating my love for life and finding my way out of a storm.

In preparation of publishing a new edition of *climate* I found myself faced with a task few writers want to face: rereading my previous work. It had been over a year since I revisited this book in its entirety. So, I did what all the best (or maybe worst) writers do. I procrastinated. I stared at the copy of *climate* on my bookshelf, and I deep cleaned my kitchen, took a walk, scrolled on the internet. I did anything other than open this book.

I told myself that I was avoiding it because I am a changed person now. I told myself that that I was running because I had outgrown the version of myself who wrote it.

It turns out that as well as being a talented procrastinator I can also be a talented liar.

The honest reason for my avoidance was quite the opposite. What I was most afraid of was that time had passed, and I hadn't changed. I was afraid that reopening this book would be like reopening an old wound. What if some part of me is still as lost as I was when I wrote these poems?

I would like to say that I was wrong. I would like to say that I do not recognize myself in these pages. But saying that would void the integrity of this entire book. One of my key intentions with *climate* was to remind myself that it is normal to cycle through various weather conditions. Meaning is derived from journeying through both the sun and the rain.

As I write this introduction, I find myself once again in a season of great change and stormy weather. As I revisit these pages, I *do* see myself staring back at me. I *have* grown and changed, but life has a way of teaching us the same lessons over again in different ways.

As difficult as it may be to look my past self in the eyes, there is something comforting in the way life parallels itself. There is solace in knowing I have been here before and the clouds eventually passed.

So, as you find your way through this book, this is the message I hope to impart to you: change *is* inevitable and deeply uncomfortable. But instead of fighting the change, I hope you allow yourself to feel it all. Learn the same lessons over and over if you need to. Let go and let go and let go until you really do. Storms tend to find their way of coming back around, but eventually so too must the sun.

So too must the sun.

stormy

you did not cause this storm
the storm was always inside me
you just set it loose

probably friends
possibly lovers
but definitely not nothing

those were the three thoughts in my mind
the first time your path crossed mine.
when i saw those eyes for the first time.

then i learned your favorite color,
realized how easily you paint a smile
across my serious disposition.
I started practicing learning you.
thinking about you a little too much
in my spare time.
then the three thoughts changed.

probably lovers
possibly friends
but definitely not nothing

then things began to change.
i realized the love only went one way.
i started anticipating the feeling of you pulling away. your
sentences became shorter
as my grip became stronger
on the love that was falling from my fingertips.
you took my smile as easily as you had given it.
the three thoughts chimed one more time.

probably nothing
possibly friends
but definitely not lovers

i wasn't happy
but i was with you
and truthfully
happiness was the least of the things
i would sacrifice
to love you

i know that i'm supposed to put myself first
but i *was* putting myself first
because what i wanted more than anything
was to be yours

what if you thought
they were everything?

what if it felt like the galaxies had whispered
your names in the same breath?

what if they
became your person?

what if they learned every bit of you
and you learned every little piece of them?

what if they became
all your future plans?

and what if
it ends?

tell me,
what then?

even after you broke my heart
you tried to make me smile and laugh
you hated to see me hurt
that is the most devastating kind of heartbreak

the kind where you both still care

there is a part of me that will always be yours.

one of the scariest feelings
is watching a person outgrow you

as if you are an old pair of shoes
that they wore a bit too long.
you're stuck in what once was
and they're ready to move on.

slowly the person you met
only exists inside your head.
you can't help fighting for a love
that has long been pronounced dead.

love requires that we grow together
you along with me,
but truth be told sometimes in love
you begin to grow separately.

i always leave the party early
just to hear someone ask me to stay
i always leave love early
so that i can hear the same

truthfully, I crave a love
who doesn't play my game
and notices my presence
before I've walked away.

i think when the universe rolled the dice
it put your name on one side
and put mine on the other
and though the dice could roll
a hundred thousand times
your name will never end up
landing next to mine
~*cruel game*

hand-holding is a mutual activity
no matter how tightly you grasp
there will always be something you lack
if they do not hold you back

i never wanted to be your first choice
being your first choice
implies that there is a second choice
i wanted to be your *only* choice

for once i wanted someone to be so sure of me
that everything else disappears.

it costs me so much more than my love to love you.

they don't see it all
the people who are telling you
to let it go

all they see
is the destruction of a broken relationship
they see the tears and fights and frustration
they see all the ugly broken parts
they see what is left

they don't see how the ruins were once a castle
the rubble was once a masterpiece
this love wasn't always so broken

it's easy to tell you to walk away
when they can't see all you're walking away from

i didn't know it was possible
to suffer the weight of forever
in a moment
but that was how it felt
looking at you for the last time

the worst of it all
is that i understand exactly why
you had to go

the worst of it all
is that i can never feel my pain
without feeling yours first

the worst of it all
is that i can't hate you
because i know every reason
you did what you did

the worst of it all
is that i can't be angry
because my anger is always
accompanied by guilt

i'm so tired of being wise
sometimes i just want to be hurt.

they told me my job description
but i think i've got it wrong.
they said i was supposed to man the lighthouse
and save lost ships from going down.

but every time i saw the ships
i forgot about the light.
i dove headfirst into the sea
and swam to save their life.

i drowned us both in the process;
the ships never found the shore.
i ended up helping less
when i meant to be helping more.

i think when they told me
to save people with my light,
i mistook their words
and tried to save people with my life.

i know i should have turned the light on,
i know i should have taken their advice,
but i don't know what love is
if it is not sacrifice.

i wish i knew how to fight for me
the way i fight for you

it happened
the clouds rolled in again
you know them
you know what to do
you wait
just like you have before
and time will carry them away again

sometimes i wake
with shadows in my veins
that don't allow me to move

they seep into my bones
they fog my vision
they linger all day long

your silence
is the loudest noise
in this room

your silence screams
"i don't love you anymore"
louder than your voice ever could

now that this is over
someone else will love you

that simultaneously
comforts me
and ruins me

i wish someone warned me
how destructive empathy could be

i wish someone taught me
that i shouldn't feel for you
until after i feel for me

i'm still seeing shooting stars
and you are seeing burning rocks

i keep calling this complicated
you're calling it over

you were always one
to see things
as they are

back to being friends,
but this time
friends who know each other
a little too well

i don't want someone to fix this.

i want someone to tell me
i don't need fixing.
i want someone to tell me
the weight of life
is a reasonable excuse
to feel this heavy.

the last time my heart was this dark,
i started picking up hobbies to fill the cracks.
i had to occupy myself to cope.

this time, all i can do is sit here
in my brokenness and wonder
how much more i can possibly take.

i can't pinpoint an instant that it began
i didn't wake up one morning
with the weight of the entire sky on my shoulders

i didn't notice the clouds accumulating
until one day it started to rain
and never stopped

how do i get rid of this heaviness
when it is me?
what if
i am the rain?

i know what
"i don't want to hurt you"
means

it means
"i'm probably going to"

i can't sleep.

i can't do anything but sleep.

i tried to drink healing like it was bleach. i tried to consume
anything i thought would erase my memory.

i read books
i drowned my thoughts in music
i distracted myself by using other people
i thought that i could clean out my head
and erase the stains you left

so intently focused on removing the damage,
i forgot i was still bleeding.
it is no use trying to clean up
when you still have open wounds

i discovered that trying to force
premature healing is suppression.
trying to heal too quickly is like poison
and there is nothing more painful
than pouring bleach into open wounds.

i told her i was hurting
she didn't ask why
she didn't tell me to explain
she didn't give me any advice
she just told me it was okay
and let me cry.

sometimes we just need someone to tell us
that what we are feeling is okay.

whatever you are feeling today
it's okay.

no one is coming
to save you from yourself
the storm inside
is yours to survive

lately i wake up in the morning and already feel i've failed. i know it is confusing to you and it doesn't look like i've done a single thing, but please know that sometimes fighting looks different for me. sometimes failure doesn't require action. it only requires that i moved in my mind and my mind was not impressed with what i did.

i hate to reduce my depression down to a hypothetical happening inside my head. it is more than that. it is heavier than that. but if i can somehow make you understand half of the weight or half of the reason i can't move from my bed today then maybe i will be one step closer to breathing a little easier. if i can somehow share what it is like to be in my mind i will be one step closer to liberation. if i can make you comprehend why i feel like a failure when i haven't done a single thing,

your understanding will somehow set me free.

i wish that i didn't disappoint you
when i can't love myself.

when i can't eat
when i can't drink
when i can't take care of me.

because now there are two things
inside me screaming.
one is telling me that i am failing myself,
the other is telling me that i'm failing you.

i know that you only look at me that way
because you love me
but you don't understand
it tears me twice apart
that by being reckless with my life
i'm being reckless with your heart.

you don't have to explain it
you just have to feel it

you know that dream
where you are being chased
but can't seem to run?
you feel as if you are moving underwater
trying to get away.

that's what i feel like every day
like i can't move
and i'm always being chased.
i wish i could wake up.
~anxiety

you're taking trips to italy
with your new girl
you're introducing her to your family
they're falling in love with her
almost as quickly as you did.

i can't blame you
or her
or them
but i can't help but wonder
what it would be like
to be the girl
that gets to meet your family.

the truth about the sadness
is that it isn't invasive.
it doesn't walk in on a beautiful day
and suddenly everything becomes dim.
it is different than that.

sadness doesn't kidnap its victims
it befriends them.
it doesn't walk in forcefully and drag you down
it invites you,
tells you exactly what you want to hear:
you are safe,
there are no expectations here.
it promises you rest at the cost of happiness.

sadness does not have to beckon
i go willingly.
i can feel when i start to sink again.
i know i am not drowning,
i am allowing the water to fill the places
where i feel numb.
i find solace in silence that comes
from dark waters.

it is important not to allow it to become habitual
but sometimes
sadness ensures
that i don't lose touch with my humanity,

and for that i thank her.

existing does not always have to be a burden
allow yourself to feel the sun
give yourself permission to put down
the backpack full of stones

you weren't meant to feel this heavy

i don't want to be rescued
i just want someone to notice
that i'm trapped

the problem is
i didn't like me
before you didn't like me

you did not write the story
you only reinforced my narrative

your hatred was not the bullet
that killed me
mine was

do not fight yourself
there are enough battles
without becoming your own adversary

i am more logical than i am emotional.

this means that when i do become emotional there is a part of me that cries and there is another part of me that stands on the outside, observing, examining, and critiquing. i wish for once that i could feel something without being split in two. i wish i could cry without having an inner critic to answer to.

perhaps my greatest flaw
is not that i am broken
perhaps my greatest flaw
is that i refuse to let anyone see it

you're starving yourself and you don't even realize it.
but i do.
i see the unanswered texts in your phone.
i see the way you close the doors
on the people you love.
you are depriving yourself of affection.

i know you didn't shut your doors
out of resentment. you did it out of fear.
you're scared of what's inside of you.
but i'm not.
you think you can smother yourself quietly
but you can't.

i've been counting the stars every night
and i noticed when you disappeared—
when you tried to put out your light.

i know you didn't ask for it but
here are some reasons to let love inside:

one—you deserve it
the same way you deserve to eat and drink
you are worthy of all the love
in a thousand galaxies

two—you are you. the universe only ever witnessed one of you and that's all we will ever get. please let the world return to you at least half of what you give.

three—most importantly, all the reasons you believe you are unlovable are all the reasons you need love. love will heal you in the places closed doors won't.

stop starving yourself of love.
please text your people back.
you are deserving.

all the parts you think are broken or missing,
love will put them back.

why can't you tell me something good for once?
~*conversations with my brain*

when you're driving a car and it starts running out of gas, the car doesn't slow down. not until the tank is completely empty does everything shut down. i think for a long time i was a car with the gas light on. always on the edge of breaking down but still running full speed into disaster. no one knew that anything was wrong, until one day, i just stopped. stopped getting out of bed, stopped answering the phone, stopped caring.

everyone asked what happened
but they didn't know
i'd been on empty for weeks.

i took an eraser and erased myself today.
i like it better when i think of it that way,
as if i was only a name on a page
not a real person with real feelings
and real consequences when i leave.

i wonder sometimes
what the sunrise looked like
the day after i died.
i wonder what song
played on the radio the next day.
i think about anything
not to imagine the pain on your face.

but i see it now
and i see how i've shattered you
and there is nothing i can do.
i can't rewrite myself into the story.
i can't see the sunrise i wonder about.
i can't listen to the radio
with one hand out the window.
i can't fix this
i'm sorry.

i took an eraser and erased myself today
i like it better when i think of it that way
but truthfully it's not so simple
or inconsequential to disappear

there are people left behind
there is music left to hear

i can feel panic rising
and i don't know the source
how do i close the floodgates
if i can't see past the waves?

perhaps the nighttime hurts
because in the dark
we are forced to face
everything we can't see

the lights dim
and there is nothing
to distract me
from the fact
that you're gone

the worst part about having a sickness
that exists only within my head
isn't that no one else can see it.
it's that i can't see it either.

it's that i'm unsure whether i believe myself
when i say that something feels off between my ears. i am
constantly pleading a case with my own consciousness to
prove that i am unwell.

but well people
do not try to prove to themselves that they are sick.
well people
do not question if they are well.
well people
aren't constantly try to dissect themselves.

when will i let my unwellness
be proof of my unwellness?
when will i let my ache
be evidence of my ache?

i do not need you
to believe me when i say that i am unwell.
for once
i just want to believe myself.

i pretend i'm searching
for something new
when really
i'm just looking for you

i hate that the wound i sustained from you
bleeds into everything else i do.
i hate that every new lover
immediately turns red.

before i have held their hand,
i know exactly how it will feel
when they pull away from me.

and i always assume they will.

in moment of great loss or immense grief it becomes impossible to comprehend how life continues. it feels as if the world should stop spinning on its axis. the sun should be scolded for shining. and all should be still to witness the brokenness of your heart.

but that is not what happens

however inconsiderate it seems the sun continues to shine the world continues to turn and life persists. despite your resistance the current of life continues.

so too will you.

they don't send ambulances
for broken hearts,
just broken bodies.

when help doesn't come
we assume we must break our own bones
we must make the outside
reflect how it feels within.

maybe then they'll send help
maybe then they'll listen
maybe then they'll believe us
when we say we hurt.

why can't the evidence of my ache
be the way i feel?
why does blood have to spill
to make my pain look real?

i don't think the world should wait
for people to puncture their skin
to worry about the trouble within.

i wish we treated broken hearts
like broken bones
and sent ambulances
for bleeding souls.

you are not too damaged to love

you are not too damaged to love

you are not too damaged to love

someone made a mistake
when choosing the soundtrack for my movie.
they gave me plenty of happy scenes,
but sad music consistently
plays in the background.

i'm living this contradiction.
i should be happy
but the tragic music in my mind
is too loud.
all is well
but the painful melody persists.

how i *should* feel
constantly wars
with how i *do* feel
and the symphony inside
always wins.

you can always come back to me
that is the beauty of hiding myself in a book
if you need me
you can find me here

sincerely,
your friend between the pages

self-destruction is circular.

i tear myself down
get inside my head and remind myself
that i am unworthy and unlovable.
i take my pain out on my own body and mind.

then i step back and look
at the damage done.
i have no one to blame but myself.

so, it starts again
blame becomes anger,
anger becomes destruction,
and i become the victim of myself.

i have nowhere to place the knife
other than my own skin.
i keep tearing myself down
to avenge my own devastation.
i'm tired of playing both sides of the chess game.

the circle will only cease
when i learn to forgive myself,
when i can accept that
i will never be perfect
when i surrender
in a war where the enemy

is me.

"why would you want to live somewhere it rains all the time?"

"because for once the world around me looks like the world inside me."

i think i've been sad
for longer than i've been alive.
i know that sounds counterintuitive
but let me explain.

all we are is energy
passed from one form of life
to the next
and before i became myself
i was something else instead.

i was a wilted flower,
or a stormy sea,
i was the last light of a dying star,
i was a fallen teardrop,
i was the final autumn leaf,
i was *i love you* whispered too late or too far.

from the start
my soul has been mourning some loss
that never belonged to me.
i am convinced that some people come into this world
carrying a bit of hand-me-down grief.

my agony sits like a bright red stop sign on my nose
i keep thinking about
the worlds i could reshape
if only i could see past my own pain

darkness is only the absence of light

so i spent my life
less afraid of the dark
and more afraid of the light.

i befriend the absence
because the one thing
darkness cannot do
that light can
is leave.

is depression the consequence of my consciousness?

is being alive anything more than my hopelessness?

i thought that my heartache
was a symptom of you leaving
but it's still here
long after you're gone

i'm starting to think
that it isn't your fault
and there's something more
that's wrong.

like maybe i've always felt unlovable
and you just reinforced my doubts.
maybe there's always been a hole in my heart
and you just turned it inside out.

finally i can see how empty it's been
and how you are not to blame
my heartache is just a symptom of existing
and you were just a player in the game

i wish i wasn't so desperate
for someone to prove to me
that i can be loved

you hurt the world
because you think it needs to pay
for the pain it handed you

i don't think
that you are evil for it,
i think that you are coping

it does not justify what you did
but you are not wrong for how you feel

you don't have to take responsibility
for every ache you feel.
it is not your fault
life is heavy.
it is not your fault
you were treated poorly.
it is not your fault
you were hurt.

your pain
is not your fault

you should not have to love with hesitation
your love isn't too much

an apology to the people who have been called
"too sad to love":

you battle the storms you do
because you carry a depth in you
that shallow souls will never understand
your depth is not a burden
it is a gift

don't worry about the destination
your only concern
is the next step.

just concentrate on jumping over
today's puddles.

when you learn to perform first aid, the first step is to make sure the victim is safe. i have discovered that healing from trauma is the same. to heal, we must find ourselves in a space where we feel safe. we cannot simultaneously mend our hearts and defend our walls. sometimes that means movement. it means leaving this place or these people behind. it means searching for new locations where the storms inside you finally feel at rest. then—and only then—can you open your suitcase, unload all you've been carrying, and sort through the past. only when your heart is safe can you finally let it lie.

seek shelter first.

when life feels out of control
find comfort in all that stays the same
the sun still rises
the seasons remain
the air is filled with a familiar fresh aroma
every time it rains
when the world feels like it is collapsing
remember that
some things do not change

you must give yourself
the nutrients to grow

growth does not simply
happen to you;
it is a result

on the days
when the little things
become too much
and even the smallest movement
requires the greatest strength

you are not fragile
you are not weak
you are climbing mountains
that nobody sees

strength is not only walking away. it is shaking hands with whatever you are leaving because you have made peace with that disaster.

leave the tempest out of your freedom, not your fear.

foggy

i woke up one day
and the rain had gone away
but the clouds descended from above
and fogged up my brain

now i don't know where to go
i cannot see my way
when i look into the mirror
i cannot find my face

i don't want to be friends
with the person i've been lately

i don't want to think about love anymore. or at least i don't want to think about it in the way i did before. i've been making myself sick waiting for the perfect love story. i'm done poking needles in my skin trying to inject love into my veins. i want to stop chasing people and affection. instead, i want to start soaking in the earth and the sunlight until i become a walking painting of love that is not forced.

there is love in this world that will simply seep into your veins. there is love you don't have to hurt yourself to receive.

learn to contend with your question marks
learn to accept what wasn't
but could have been

there are times in life where we aren't really moving toward a destination. we hover in the hallway of existence. gazing at the photos on the wall. we wait in the space between our memories and our future.

remember that there is purpose in this too. there is time to rest in the hallway and wait for the next door to open. we don't always have to be anxious or impatient for tomorrow. be grateful for the time you've been given to heal, grow, and regroup before this next chapter starts.

one moment
i am bold
and so sure of myself
you could balance skyscrapers
on my confidence

the next moment
the skyscraper falls
and my insecurities scatter
like broken glass across the floor

why is it all so fragile?

you must shut it all off
silence the background noise
so you can hear your heart.

i realized i was doing everything wrong
the day that someone told me
that my problems
were becoming my personality

as much as that hurt to hear
it was true

sometimes
it becomes necessary
to spend time
in the uncomfortable corners
of your mind.

one of the most terrifying experiences
is when you lose the feeling of feeling entirely.
when the sparks that used to ignite you
simply ricochet off your skin
like waterlogged kindling.
every day seems to compound into a single impression of an
uneventful existence.

i think that is the reason
we cling to the people and places that damage us.
i would much rather spend the night with misery than spend
the night alone.

when the sun sets
and i'm just tired enough
to forget i'm better off without you
i reach back to the place inside me
that you haven't quite departed yet
and i relive a life you left behind
and i reimagine a future where you didn't go

i want the little things back.
it's not the big picture anymore.
it's breakfast with you.
it's you allowing the sunlight
to soak in to your skin.
it's chocolate chip pancakes and eggs
on a green couch in my living room.
it's midday coffee shop trips
because we couldn't get out of bed.
it is wandering through bookstores,
racing you through grocery aisles
with shopping carts.
it's the creases at the corners of your eyes,
its phone calls that drag on into the night,
it's the way we said goodbye at least 8 times
because i never really wanted to leave your side.

i think we tend to let go of the small things last.
i don't need you anymore,
i just want the chocolate chip pancakes back.

you probably don't notice it,
but the world has turned 58 times
since the last time i saw you.

30 times since the day i stopped looking at
photos of us together.

and 0 times since the last time
i thought about you.

you can call it obsessive
but i call it self-control.
because if i really said
all the things i wanted to say,
we would be here until the earth stopped turning.

to me, doing laps around the earth's core
is not a race i feel capable of running without you
and sometimes it takes everything in me
not to pick up the phone and call.

but i don't. because if i am going to spin
out of control, i am going to do it with someone who
notices every single shift the world makes without me
and every sunrise they watch
when i'm not by their side.

i'm going to find someone who uses me
to calculate time.

even though
i am happy for you
there are still obvious gaps between my fingers
where i know yours would fit perfectly.

even though
i know we will never end up together,
i still have lighthearted arguments with my soul about letting
you go.

even though
i feel a little heavier sometimes
now that you aren't mine,

even though
there was a time
where we were sure
where i swore i saw forever in your eyes,

even though
we loved each other
but lost the fight,

in the end i'm okay
with the way you had to go,
and i want you to know
that i can be content
with you being my
"even though."

sometimes i imagine
the me i would have been
if we had never met

and she appears so much lighter
and she floats instead of walking
and she wears the color yellow
and she doesn't hesitate to speak
and she writes poetry about blue skies
and listens to music with fewer string instruments

and although she is lighter
i'm not so sure that i like her
or that she really knows herself

so if it took losing you
to meet myself truly
i suppose i should thank you
if only for this

i've never really looked great in yellow
and i'm a bit partial to my violins

i don't want to be looked at
if you are not here to see my soul

there is so much of me to behold

i don't want to be looked at,
i want to be seen.

sane love makes you feel insane
if insane love is all you have ever known

patient love makes you feel restless
if restless love is all you have ever known

gentle love makes you feel uneasy
if uneasy love is all you have ever known

peaceful love makes you feel anxious
if anxious love is all you have ever known

we are creatures of the love that we know
the way we are accustomed to receiving love
defines the love that we search for

the worst kind of homesickness
is the kind where you just want to get back
to yourself

people care much less about logic
than they think they do.

the likelihood of getting in a plane crash is about 1 in 11 million.
regardless, the first time i boarded an airplane statistics became
like fairy tales. the only number i cared about was the time
that this hell ship would land and i could put my feet back on
the ground. now i've probably been on at least 50 planes. i
usually trust that i will land safely. the statistics didn't change,
but my feelings about flying did. it is not the numbers that
lead to my trust in flight. it is my experience.

it's the same with my trust in people.
i know your statistics are great, but my experience isn't the
same.

i know it's not fair, and the facts are all there, but it's going to
take a few flights before i can relax. it might take a couple
smooth landings before i can trust you.

the fact of the future
is that you do not know
until you know.

don't beat yourself up over things you didn't know until you knew them. that person you should not have handed your trust to so readily, those things you probably shouldn't have said, that disaster you could have averted. the world doesn't always hand out red flags. it doesn't give receipts for lessons we learned too late. so, we move forward, and we do the best that we can with the knowledge that we hold now.

i wish you would let
some of the love you give
soak into your own bloodstream

i started looking at letting go differently, because letting go of you was something that felt impossible. it was like trying to forget the lyrics to your favorite song; you can stop listening to the music on repeat but as soon as you hear it again, every word comes flooding back.

i realize now that forgetting and letting go aren't necessarily the same. although i can't make myself forget the lyrics, i can stop singing along. no amount of time will remove this tune from my veins, but i can find new music. i'm coming to terms with the fact that the memories i made with you may be permanent but my misery is not.

contentment feels like letting my guard down
peace feels like a risk

i used to think that no one could understand me.

i prided myself on my individuality so much that it resulted in a deep loneliness. my internal conversation persuaded me to believe any feeling that i felt, i was experiencing entirely alone. i did not think that i could be simultaneously complex and comparable to others.

what i called individuality was actually isolation.

so, if you are the kind of person who likes to put yourself on an island, understand that it is possible to keep your identity even when sharing yourself. you do not lose your complexity just because you are understood. your ability to relate to others is a gift that should not be sacrificed for your pride.

you are intricate.
you are complex.
the soul is a unique topographic image depicting your highs and your lows.
you do not have to isolate yourself
to prove that.

there is time for you here

there is time for you to be unsure about the future
there is time for you to decide on your dreams
there is time to change your mind when you realize those
dreams weren't everything you wanted
there is time to find closure
for wounds that took a little longer to heal
there is time for you to find love
and realize it wasn't right
even though it was real
there is time for you to change
and to grow
and to wait

you're right on time
you're not running late

know the difference between being kind
and giving too much to the wrong people
~stop watering weeds

you forgot my birthday
because you were busy
falling in love with someone new
i know we don't talk much anymore
and i thought i was done expecting things
from you.
but it turns out
birthday candles
were the last part of us
that was still burning.

i blew them out.

when i look into her eyes
it's as if she has lived a thousand lives
i can see them all locked away
begging for me
to ask her to speak
~*reflection*

who were you before all of this?

the funny thing about fading
is that so often,
no one knows it's happening
but you

no one notices
when you disappear
s   l   o   w   l   y

i hate to say it
but nothing has changed
i write all these lines about how i'm over you
but the truth is
i know i would fall back into your arms
the instant you allowed it

does that make me weak?

when i look at us in snapshots
photos saved in my phone
it appears perfect

but when i consider
who you really are
and who i really am

i realize you and i
might be better apart

it's not that i can't trust someone new
it's that i can't trust myself anymore
and that
is so much worse

you do not have to carry the weight
of what someone else is feeling

you do not have to carry the weight
of what someone else is expecting

you do not have to carry the weight
of what someone else is experiencing

the clouds are parting outside
but it is still dark in here

let me make mistakes
let me miss my alarm
let me trip over my shoelaces
let me fail tests
let me be clumsy
and weird
and ugly
and imperfect
~from me to me

i don't try to read your mind anymore
i don't think about what you might be thinking
i never knew the freedom i was sacrificing
by spending more time in your mind
than my own

i'm not sad about it anymore
and i'm not sure what to do with that
~*empty*

i looked up at the stars and asked them how to become strangers with someone i once loved.

they didn't answer.

sometimes i think the healing is in the questioning. it's facing the things that frighten you. like the way i may never be able to unlearn you or untrace your features with my fingertips.

i think sometimes asking the sky what is next for me is all the progress that i need. the first step to finding your way is admitting that you are lost. there may not be a map written in the stars. there may be a long journey ahead, but looking up and asking *what now?* might be the first step.

"why do you feel like you need to save everyone?"

"because i know what it is like to need saving."

"what if no one needs to be saved?"

"someone always needs saving."

perhaps the problem
is that you aren't starting in the right place
you're getting ahead of yourself
please tie your shoes
before you run headlong
into the wind

i'm learning
that true happiness
is not merely the absence
of my sadness

i let it go. i got over her a long time ago. i don't hope that she shows up at my door. i don't hope that she calls. i've found myself in limbo because i'm not sure what to do if i'm not trying to let go of someone. i don't know where we go from here.

i've spent the past five years in and out of relationships and a large part of that time was complicated. nothing is complicated now. i began to rely on the consistency of complications to dictate my every move. it's like i spent the past five years of my life playing defense and suddenly i'm choosing my steps rather than reacting to someone else's. it is simultaneously liberating and terrifying.

there is a whole world in front of me
and finally
it's all mine.

this part of my life feels like sitting at stoplights
that never seem to change.

is my art only my pain?

am i the artist
or an impostor?

am i gifted
if i am not broken?

i put people on paper
i transform feelings into words
i make my agony two-dimensional
so that it doesn't hurt.

it's my magic.

i have a special relationship with the floor
i spend a lot of time making sure it isn't lonely.
it spends a lot of time reminding me
that the closer i am to the ground
the more room there is to rise.

i want to let the ocean swallow me
not in the *i want to drown* way
or *i want to disappear* way
but in the *i want to be one with something*
that is so much bigger than me way

i can't tell
if my expectations for love
are far too high
or far too low

i'm trying to read crop circles like morse code
hoping there's a hidden message from the earth
that it misses me when i'm gone.
~1 p.m. flight from dallas

pay attention to how you're feeling
when you're alone.

when all the distractions are set aside
what consumes you?

i'm so sick of wishing for the future
just to look back
and see the past
uncurl her fists
holding everything
i didn't know
how to love
at the time

stop worrying about the direction
that you move next
and just move
~*indecision*

"when will i ever be good enough for you?"
~to the girl in the mirror

my pain has become my only certainty
i'm afraid that if i let my soul get too light
it will float away from me

i board every airplane with the expectation that i am going to meet the love of my life.

i can't decide if that makes me romantic or stupid.

perhaps both.

it has been a year
the fear still rests in my bones
losing you settled deep in my core
it convinced me
that i will never be able to love
like i could before

it taught my hands to hesitate
it taught me to keep my heart to myself
it filled me with doubt
and emptied me of everything else

it's been a year
and although i don't miss you anymore
i miss when it wasn't so hard
to open my doors

empty rooms are the most powerful
it is not the substance that makes anything incredible
it is the potential

emptiness is not a state of despair
it is a state of possibility

please stop looking for love
when it is all around you

you haven't yet understood
the language of the universe

light is the love language of the stars
warmth is the love language of the sun
movement is the love language of the wind
steadiness is the love language of the mountains

if you listen well enough
they will remind you
there *is* love.

there's this battle that wars within me
between independence and reliance.
it feels impossible to hold both simultaneously.

it is as if I must choose
between independent and alone
or dependent and loved.

loneliness is always
a topic of conversation in my body
as if even my bones know
how long it has been
since someone loved me beyond my scars

i want to be okay alone
but i'm not

stop shopping for love and paying for it with your ability to conform to the needs of others.

let love come to you. and when it does, you will not have to reinvent yourself to keep it.

i told myself
i was running from love
because i was better on my own.
but i think i am running
because deep down,
i'm afraid i am unlovable

i'm tired of testing my theory
and watching people walk away.
the evidence thus far
is overwhelming.
i can't experiment
with my heart anymore.

something you must realize
is that the more you value yourself
the lonelier you become.

when you become picky
about who you share yourself with,
it can feel discouraging.
it may tempt you to shrink yourself
so that you can fit back into the palms
of people who did not value you.
your desire may tease you with affection
at the cost of your worth.
it may beg you to smother your starlight
back into dust.

please be patient.
loneliness is deceptive
in the way it convinces its victims
that it is eternal.

keep waiting
for hands that are not afraid
of holding the stars.

i hunger to meet a lover
who leaves neither
my head or my heart
longing for more

sunny

when it finally hits you,
feel it
feel all of it
do not hide yourself in the shade
run toward it
sit in it
absorb it
breathe it in
become it
~sunlight

i like to think of my heart
as a hermit crab
that recently outgrew its shell.

in order to move forward
you must leave something behind.

in order to find a new home
you must shed your protection.

in order to love again
you must take down the wall.

i'm not going to pretend i don't miss you sometimes. but recently, i've been reminded of who i used to be and i can't let her slip though my fingers again.

if i must let you go
to have her
i will choose her every time.

the sky never breaks my heart.

"childish" they called me.

"jealous?" i replied, laughing and stomping in a puddle.

"if being childish is being in love with the ordinary,
i sincerely hope that i never grow up."

when i tell people i am an artist
they usually ask to see my paintings

when i tell people my art is words
they say never mind

i want to tell them
my art creates paintings too

my words are the paint
and the canvas is your mind

it's not embarrassing or weak
or needy or anything but human
to desire love.

small cure for loneliness:

buy plants. every time you wake say to them,
"good morning, plants, you look beautiful today."

if you listen well enough, they will reply. their love will speak
in colorful blossoms or tiny new leaves.

"there's a reason you can't stop thinking about me"

sincerely,
the dreams you've been ignoring

i think that so often we try to disconnect
our bodies and our minds
but in reality
we are the synchronicity of both

for one to move
we must move both
for one to change
we must change both
for one to heal
we must heal both

sometimes we confuse missing a moment for missing a person. when i push replay it's the same scenes i see again and again. the truth is, those few moments of happiness are not you.

they are only a piece of you that i've frozen in time and used to convince myself that somewhere out there, that version of us could still exist. but it can't.
i am clinging to a moment, a snapshot, a memory that is not subject to change.

i'm learning to accept that people may come back into your life, but no one has the privilege of bargaining with time. so, even if you walked back though this door,

i won't expect a person to be a memory.
i won't keep replaying moments of my life.
i must learn to live in this one.

you give yourself
even when you feel
you have nothing left to give

so even if no one else tells you—
thank you for being so strong

how dare you
look at the rain and call it beautiful
how dare you
listen to the thunder and call it magnificent
how dare you
admire the beauty around you
while disregarding the magnificence
that runs through your veins.
believe me when i say
that thunderstorms are afraid of your power.

underneath all these pieces you dare deem
unworthy or unlovable
you are untouchable,
royalty of a universe that is all your own.

you have the power to craft masterpieces
with only your imagination.

so before you look in the mirror
and believe that you are anything less than artistry
i hope in the back of your head you hear me.

when your eyes meet your insecurities
please let these words echo through:
how dare you.

being understood is my love language. i suppose that is why i look for pieces of myself in someone else. that is also the reason i get so excited when i meet someone whose favorite ice-cream flavor is cookie dough or who is just as in love with the sky as i am. the way to love me is to remind me that i am not alone.

perhaps that is a little true for all of us.

did you know when you look up the word "heart"
in the dictionary
there are 6 different definitions?
i think that that is the very reason
i remain in love with humanity.

it is so characteristic of us
to take an organ used for pumping blood and say
to me it means this
and to me it means something else.

i love that we designed our language
so that i can tell you
that i hope your heart is okay
and that could mean
the beat in your chest
or the tears that pile up behind your eyes.

i am infatuated with the way
we assign hearts to inanimate objects too;
you know exactly where to meet me
if i tell you i'm in the heart of the room.
when i speak about your heart
i can mean your disposition, your intentions,
your nature, or your core.

i love the way
we decided there was room for more
in our hearts
than blood.

stop searching for meaning
it means something
because it means something to you
it matters
because it matters to you
it is important
because it is important to you
it is
because
you are
and that is enough.

freedom is choosing to stop worrying about letting others down and exclusively holding yourself accountable for the expectations you set for yourself.

on average there are about two shooting stars in the sky per hour. this might come as a surprise because we often think that seeing a shooting star is rare. most of us only see a few in our lifetime. i think that falling in love is a lot like that. it is important to recognize how rare it can be. but it is also important not to forget that no matter how rare the love that you lost, there is always more for you out there.

just keep looking up.

there is an undeniable emphasis that we all place on love. it is the only thing that is logically entirely unnecessary for life, yet we continue to seek it as if it is the last breath of oxygen before drowning.

but why?

this is the conclusion that i have come to. humans are at their best when they are loved. it elicits a part of us that is selfless and confident. if we are loved well, we are ambitious and sure of ourselves. i have also found this. the same can result from love that is attained internally. when you love who you are, you become your best. you become selfless and confident. you become ambitious and sure of yourself. this is not to say that love from others is unnecessary. rather it is to say it is necessary to find vitality within yourself.

you do not have to be isolated,
but you must be sustained by your own breath first.

one of my favorite parts of the day
is when i shower
and put on my hoodie that is three sizes too big.

the part of my day
where i pile myself with blankets
and let my bed absorb
the weight of my worries.

the part of the day
when the nighttime
has just kissed the surface of the earth,
when the turmoil inside me
begins to settle like a glass lake.
i close my eyes
and sink into myself.

i think i'm waiting for someone whose love makes me feel
like that time of day.

i'm waiting for someone's arms
to be my hoodie that is three sizes too big.
i'm waiting for someone's chest
to absorb the weight of my worries.
when the nighttime
has just kissed the surface of the earth
when the turmoil inside me
begins to settle like a glass lake
i close my eyes
and sink into them.

perhaps your chaos
is your magic

some things you should know
about loving me:

i will take some time to trust you
my heart is a little black-and-blue
from hands that were
a little too clumsy to hold it
i keep myself a bit hidden
i keep my walls a bit high

but when they fall
you won't have to remind me of your birthday
i hold in my heart
freckle counting
text me when you're home
call me when you need me
kind of love

i won't let you
have a single doubt in your mind
that the love song stuck in my head
says anything but your name
because the thing about having a heart
with walls around it
is that once you're let inside
it makes a rather safe place
to stay

i am watching entire mountains
fit into the tiny frame of my oval window
and i am certain
that everything
is going to be okay
~4 p.m. flight to chicago

maybe getting better
isn't a cosmic shift
it's just waking up every day
and trying

ants are small to humans
humans are small to stars
stars are small to galaxies

everything is relative
so you choose your narrative
you choose how significant you are

your
presence
is
making
a
difference

sincerely,
the world

there is space for what you give the universe
there is space for your tears
there is space for your laughter
there is space for what you create
there is space for you

take up that space

no one ever looks at the stars
and wishes they were gone.
no one ever asks the ocean
why it stays so long.

no one wishes the moon away
they don't ask for it to disappear.
no one is unkind to the sun
we know it's needed here.

no one ever questions
the existence of these things.
we accept that they are exactly
what they are meant to be.

so don't you dare look in the mirror
and wish that you were gone.
do not ask yourself
why you've stayed so long.

don't wish yourself away
don't ask to disappear.
don't be unkind to yourself
please know we need you here.

do not question your existence
you are everything.
please accept that you are
exactly what you are meant to be.

you don't have to prove to me
that you are worthy of my love

sincerely,
myself

you were the love of my life
until someone else was

i know that someone will love
the darkness in me
because of how fiercely
i loved the darkness in you.

i will not ask for love.
because the question is not
whether or not
i should be loved.
it's who i should be loved by.

if you are the kind of person
that i must ask to love me,
then you are not the kind of person
that is meant to.

i don't think any artist knows they're creating a famous masterpiece when they create it. some of them die believing that their life's work was worthless just for their piece to be hung on the walls of museums for years to come. my point is,

i don't think you realize what a masterpiece you are. the world gives us inadequate assessments of the work of geniuses every day. so, if you're feeling overlooked and underappreciated, if you're feeling like this isn't the role you were assigned, it's probably because the way you're painted is a little ahead of their time.

life has taught me to be skeptical of everything. so today i am going to be skeptical of my doubt. i am going to be skeptical of the voice that tells me i don't matter. i am going to challenge the idea that i am anything but remarkable.

today i question the storm.

reclaim the power you have
over the state of your mind

sometimes i look in the mirror and count my freckles. i never finish counting. there is so much of me to discover and anyone who walked away gave up too soon.

she is everything
in all the right places
she is me

to the person i once loved:
i hope you find what you're looking for
and not in a passive-aggressive way.

i hope that the world fills you
with all that i couldn't.
perhaps it is better to say,
i hope that you find all
that is meant to fill you now
as i was meant to once.

i hope you hold hands with people
who make your heart race.
i hope you find yourself lost
in someone else's wishing well eyes.
i hope occasionally you smile
when she reminds you a little bit of me.

i hope that you don't cling to what was
and you soak yourself in everything
that right now has to offer.
i hope that every so often
you find use for the lessons
we taught each other
and you find love for the way we
grew together
then grew apart.

to the person i once loved:
i hope you find what you're looking for.

i laid in the field
and let the wind blow dandelion seeds
across my body
i hoped they would land
in all the cracks that life made in me
and i wished that instead of scars
i would sprout gardens
i allowed new growth
to be the glue
that resurrected me

who would have imagined
that the most productive thing
i could do today
was to put my feelings somewhere
other than my head

~art

it is not rare to have struggles
it is rare to be the kind of person
who cares when someone else does

i met somebody new
and they asked me
if i was still in love with you.
without hesitation i answered no.

although it was the truth,
it felt a little like betrayal.
and although i didn't lie,
it felt a little wrong to say.

i'm beginning to realize
that to say i do not love you now
is not to say that i never did.

i think there will always be
a loyal piece of my heart
living in the past
that still calls you mine.

to say i don't love you now
does not speak for our past.
it speaks for me,
in this moment.

i won't lie—it hurts to say
but who i was
when i loved you
isn't who i am today.

be picky.
be intentional
about the people you choose to call yours.
don't waste time on a love that is not mutual.
don't trip over your feet chasing
people that aren't for you.

be picky.
be aware of the value of your energy.
spend it doing the things that take your breath away
only walk down roads that your soul is screaming at you to
take.

be picky.
recognize the truth that this—
all of this—is temporary.
rely on the rarity of every inhale and exhale you take. allow
the anomaly of your every breath
to propel you to the realization
that not a single moment
should be wasted.

please let your scars
compel you to care

she was so busy trying to fall in love
she missed the love that already found her

she was so busy waiting
for butterflies in her stomach

she missed the butterfly
that landed on her nose

i've never begged for a job
i've never asked twice to be hired
but now i interview every night with the stars
i ask them a thousand times
if i can have the job of loving you
and if i can call you mine

i think a lot about the way the clouds move
not fast enough for us to notice
unless we are paying attention

i think that healing is a lot like that
one moment it's raining
and the next the sky is clear

you're not always sure
how things changed
but suddenly the sky is blue again

i have always been
a strong believer in magic
but not the kind that you find in fairy tales
rather the type that music and sunsets
are composed of

i think that you are made of it too

i want you
the way you want me
i think that's rare
~*mutual love*

i was so afraid of losing this moment,
of letting the smile on your face
fall through my fingers.

i wanted to hold on to it
but if there is one thing i've learned
it's that you must be gentle with happiness.
the instant you attempt to cling to it,
it changes.
happiness shape-shifts into hopelessness
in hands that try to harness it.

it will not be kept,
it does not have to stay,
forever is not its nature.
so when it comes hold it lightly
and let it go when it leaves.
learn to contend with its nature
and it will come more naturally.

i don't feel like i need to impress you to keep you here. you might not suppose that means much, but i've been fighting for people to stay for so long that i thought i forgot how to just love someone. how to just be loved; how to let my existence be enough.

thank you for helping me believe
that i have always been enough
that i don't have to be anything more
that i shouldn't feel like being loved
is something i must beg for

i was wrong about love
i thought you knew that it was right because of how quickly
you caught fire.
i thought that true love
was instantaneous and reckless.
although that may be the case sometimes,
that's not how it was with you.
when i knew it was right,
it was because i didn't want to dive in headfirst.
i didn't even want to jump.
i wanted to learn to love you as patiently as possible.
i wanted to trace each of the lines on your hand before i took
your hand in mine.
i wanted to know what scares you.
i wanted to find out all the little ways that i could care for
your heart and make you comfortable putting it in my hands.
i wanted to start with matches instead of torches.
i wanted to learn to be reckless in restraint.
i wanted to take as much time as we needed
to get this right.
sometimes
love isn't the fall.
it is the time you spend
sitting on the edge of the cliff
learning each other's souls
sometimes
patience is the purest practice of affection.

people will start to feel safe
embrace this
don't fight the comfort you get
from burying your head in their shoulder.

it's okay to rest here.

i am in love with you
because the way you're in love with life
makes me want to be in love with it too

if we measured love in time
and measured time in heartbeats

i would wrap my heart in pretty paper
and give it to you without a second thought
i would hand you all the time i have
every heartbeat on my clock

if we measured love in words
and measured words in books

i would fill a million pages
i'd write until my fingers ached
i'd fill every shelf in every library
with novels in your name

if we measured love in music
and measured music in songs

i would sing every song i know
and teach the birds to sing along
so one day when i'm out of breath
my love for you is never gone

when i say that you came to me out of the blue
i do not mean that it was a surprise that i fell for you.
i mean that i am certain
you ascended out of the ocean
or you descended from the sky.
because whatever world you came from
is so much more than mine.

i do not need you to understand
i just need you to try

i think that effort is love

i no longer wish to tiptoe
on the riverbanks of existence
i have spent far too many days
walking the edges of the water
never daring to jump in
never allowing myself
to love
to hope
to commit

today
i do not care if the current is powerful
i do not mind if the water is cold
i am diving in headfirst
i am throwing caution to the wind
let the river do its worst
i am determined to swim

if they feel like
hearing your favorite song
for the first time
don't let them go

do you ever think about the way that each breath you take traveled thousands of years to get to your lungs? every molecule of your body tiptoed into place after centuries of existing. you may be composed of stardust, and you wouldn't even know. do you ever consider the fact that your being was destined to be tied together at this moment? woven from the water that runs through streams and the pollen dust on the wings of butterflies.

when you doubt yourself, when you think that you don't belong, when you question your purpose, do you even consider how miraculous it is that you are here? the proof of your belonging, your purpose, your being, is all quite simply answered by your very presence. it is woven into you. it is in every breath of air that took thousands of years to belong to you.

you are not a question to be answered.
you simply are.
and that is enough.

while you spent your nights dreaming
i spent mine trying to absorb you
attempting to take captive your essence
and carry it with me when the sun rises

i do not count sheep at night
i count the ways that i can keep you

what makes your love so special
is that it isn't something profound.
it is uncomplicated.
it is easy.
it's flowers just because
it's tacos for breakfast
and make sure you text me
when you make it home safe.
it isn't anxious or impatient.
for so long i clung to this misconception
that love had to be chaotic.
i thought that the only love that was powerful was one that
was out of control.

you are not a storm,
you are not chaos,
you are love.
and i was wrong.

you say that you're not good at much
but i've never seen someone love
the way you do

and i think that is the greatest good
a person can ever be

i refuse to believe that the words *i love you* are like birthday cake. three words, reserved for special occasions, only to be given out topped with candles and frosting at the perfect moment.

i use the words *i love you* casually, and recklessly at times. but i've found that birthday cake is better at midnight and i love you is better when you don't hesitate, when you don't wait for an occasion to say it.

so here it is,

i love you.

not in the special occasion kind of way.

in the coffee in the morning on a tuesday kind of way. i love you in chalk on a sidewalk, in little post-it notes, and in extra smiles when you come home. i love you in the language of everyday things.

in seeing you at the end of each day,
in listening to every word you say.
i love you in the language of birthday cake
when it's nobody's birthday.

i've never been one to expect blue skies
i've never been one to anticipate the best.
that makes trust difficult for me.
that makes placing my hope in people impossible.
this is how i knew you were special.

the moment i met you,
trust became easy.
anticipating the best wasn't so difficult for me.
i've never met someone who's very nature
drew sunlight from within me.

the moment i met you,
i started anticipating skies that were blue.
everything that was difficult for me
became easy when i was with you.

a flower that is admired often
does not become more beautiful
in the same way
a flower that is never seen
does not become less extraordinary

attention is not a fair measurement of beauty

i finally found a book
that i couldn't put down
but this time, this book was a person
and i wanted you to know
that i've only started chapter one
but i already know that i would read this book again
and again
and again
i might even bend the pages on my favorite parts though i've
been told
you're not supposed to do that

if there is anything i've learned
it's that love doesn't care about rules

i know that all books come with endings
but endings are the least of the things
i would risk to love you
endings are the last on the list
of things that will never scare me away

because i finally found a book
that i couldn't put down
and if it's alright with you
i think i'd like to keep what i've found

to simply call her pretty
is to call the ocean a puddle
don't underestimate
her depth

i shared my favorite song with you
and i know that you weren't aware
but that was my way of saying i love you
because every feeling music floods me with
i wanted you to feel it too

it wasn't love at first sight

that isn't to say
that i was not mesmerized when i met you
but rather it is to say that there was something far more
captivating than the way you looked

i didn't fall in love when i found you
i fell in love with what i found in you

they say that love is complicated
but it's not complicated
people are complicated
love is simple

it is making two cups of coffee in the morning
instead of one
it is "text me when you get home"
"call me when you need to"
listening without saying a word

it is "this song reminds me of you"
it is "i understand how you feel"
and "with you i become a little bit more real"

it is inventing a million reasons to keep talking
even though it's late at night
it's using "see you later"
as a substitute for goodbye

don't get me wrong
love is effort
love is not ease
but it isn't quite as complicated
as they want you to believe

let me see you broken
let me see you bleeding
let me see you crying
let me see you at your worst

let me love you broken
let me love you bleeding
let me love you crying
let me love you at your worst

in case you were wondering
there is a love
that will offer you both independence and support
there is a love that holds you
without pinning your wings down
there is a love that simultaneously stops your heart and makes
it easier to breathe
you do not have to be alone to grow

can we get dressed up in the kind of clothing
that royalty wears?
can we eat fancy food?
can we run through fields of tall grass?
can we pretend that we own this kingdom?

can we get dressed down?
can we put on oversized t-shirts?
can we put on all gray and go for a drive in the rain?
can we get wrapped up in blankets
and listen to pretty music?
can we be the kings and queens of blanket forts?

i've ruined relationships
because of unrealistic expectations

this time
i recognize my tendency
to focus on myself

you are you
and i am me
and i will be grateful
for the parts of you
that you decide to share

she said i love you
the words were the same
as all the *i love you*s i had heard before.
except it was as if she spoke to me
in another font,
one that was more exquisite.
the words curled from her lips
in a way that gently persuaded me to trust them.
she spoke the phrase
but it was as if she had inscribed it on my heart
with her own handwriting.

I love you.

i like to think of life like i am walking along a beach
collecting moments shaped like seashells
and each one is unique

every shell has a story to tell
and every once in a while
i find one that is extra special

it is shaped differently
or it is bright blue
i think that one of those seashells
was the moment i met you

you're nothing like me
in the best way possible

~*magnets*

if i die today
i think this would be my parting advice:

live in this moment and love with no restraints. realize that
taking life slowly and absorbing the small things is not
wasting time. drink the coffee one sip at a time and spend
the extra 15 minutes on the phone with your best friend.

do not worry so much about the weather.

don't take it all so seriously
but if you take something seriously
let it be this.
this is not a rehearsal.
this is not a practice run.
this is not a test.
this is your life.

do not disregard how rare it is.

she speaks about the stars
as if she has held hands with each of them
and learned their deepest desires

never let go of a person
who puts one hand in yours
and stirs the galaxies with the other

there is little value
in the good you do
because it is easy
but the good you do
despite the difficulty
is priceless

kindness demands more
than your leftovers

stop chasing me with nets
and trying to hold me down with pins
i am meant to be free
~to the butterfly collector

i was accepted
they called me pretty
they called me perfect
they called me theirs

and i hated myself

i never felt more empty
than when the majority called me loved

i can never seem
to capture in words
the way that you look to my eyes

but this is how
i would encapsulate you
if i had to try

the stars came down
and kissed the earth
and left some light behind

and somehow that light
turned into you
and somehow you became mine

now every night
i thank the stars
that you are in my life

how fortunate i am
to hold the stars
when i hold your hand in mine

i am in love with people
who don't cover their window on airplanes
~cloud walkers

you undressed me with your eyes
not in the way others did before.
you weren't searching beneath my clothing
for your satisfaction.
you were searching beyond my facade
for my soul.
that is the first time someone
tried to find me that way.
you were the first
to search me further than my skin.
~*redefining naked*

goodness is gravity
the right people
will pull you

you leave me empty in all the best ways
empty of the doubt
that no one will be able to love me
empty of the certainty
that i will always be a little bit short
of what someone is looking for
empty of all the things
i was never meant to be full of

so much time i wasted looking
for someone to make me feel full
i never realized that being emptied
was always what i needed more

please claim your space in the universe
dress yourself with intention
wake up and scream to the world
"i am here"

i have a theory
that people are made of stars
because we often underestimate
all that we are

we perceive ourselves small
like dust in the sky,
when in reality
we are not tiny lights

we are powerful masses
of fire and flame
and the void flinches
at the sound of our name

i have a theory
that people are made of stars
stop being timid
the sky is ours

don't let your eyes deceive you
clocks are not circular
and you're never going to live
this 2 p.m. on a thursday again

there is no such thing
as an ordinary moment

i think the reason
they tell you
to soak in the sunlight
is because it is possible
to be drenched in light
the same way
you were once
drenched in rain

if i fail at everything else
but succeed at love
that is enough

you are my sunshine
for today.

maybe not forever
but for today.

climate

when i first chose the sections of this book, i thought that sunny would be the last one. as if joy, love, and light was the destination. but life doesn't have definitive destinations. we are constantly changing and moving. this last section is intended to help you embrace that movement. of course, there is nothing wrong with chasing the good and joy in life but there is peace in embracing that you won't always be in a sunshine state of mind.

keep going, not for the expectation of sunlight but rather for the pursuit of experiencing everything you can in this life.

i interlaced my fingers with the clouds
and attempted to pull the sky to the ground
as if i needed the clouds to rest on my shoulders
to validate how rain soaked i already felt

something strange happened
i attempted to bring the sky to me
but instead of pulling the clouds down
the clouds pulled me

they told me i didn't need them
to validate my storm or my rain
i never needed an explanation
to feel my pain

let go of what you can't control
and focus on the things you can
the rain will come
but you can carry an umbrella

welcome to my mind
i hope you are well
but if you're not
i hope somewhere in this book
you found that
your unwellness
is the same as mine

even if you will not admit it
an ember still burns within you
a light still radiates from you
a small sentence whispers within you

"i will go on"

is that not reason enough?

watch the sunset
notice how the light goes away slowly
then all at once
notice how the sky changes
from golden to blue to black

watch the sunrise
notice how the light appears slowly
then all at once
notice how the sky changes
from black to blue to golden

this is how it is meant to be
the light is meant to come and go
but never to leave entirely

my world did end when i was 16
and again when i was 18
and briefly this morning
when i couldn't move from my bed.

i do not have much hope that it will not end again
because that is the way that it is, you know?
life is riddled with endings
and change
and insufferable pain

but the other truth about endings
is that they do not come without a counterpart
every time my world has ended
it has also begun

so if i were to talk to 16 year old me
i would look her in the eyes and say i believe
that your world is collapsing
that you will never be the same.
it will collapse many more times
but the sun will rise the next day.
you will do this again
and again
and again
and maybe one day
we won't speak so much of the end

and we'll say

my world *began* when i was 16
and again when i was 18
and briefly this morning when i rose from my bed

you were poetry
before anyone wrote you
into their narrative

you were art then
and you are art now

i wish you would stop hiding
the parts of you
that you think i won't love

i traveled back in time today
i saw myself broken
on a bathroom floor
and i broke again
but this time it was different
this time it was not my pain that broke me
it was the overwhelming love i felt
for the girl who thought she was worthless
i can't wait until the day she realizes
she means everything to me
everything

i love the way you are unashamed of your humanity
i love the way you wear your worst days boldly
and you wear your best days humbly

i am the advocate of rainy days
i am the advocate for people
who cry almost as easy as they breathe
i am the advocate for the clouds that cover the sun
i am the advocate of the color gray

i went to the site of an airplane crash that happened in the 1980s
no one survived the crash

i sat in the seat where someone
had the most devastating day of their life
i cried tears for the fear that a stranger felt
i've never held more love for someone
who didn't even live in my time

for a moment
i merged hearts
with a person who became a ghost
before i even became a person

nothing but agony
could so easily
bridge the gap
of space and time

that is why
if i had the choice
i would never trade my pain

my misery
is the reason i can feel you
and yours is the reason
you can feel me

you thought my pain
was the most interesting thing about me
no one ever wanted to know
the part of me
i tried so adamantly
to hide

don't write what they want to hear

write what would destroy you if you didn't

the most beautiful and crushing part about this life is that it comes with endings. although that can be the most devastating realization, it can also be the most liberating truth. it means that no matter how big what you're facing may seem, there will be a time when this shadow passes over.

the darkness is only an eclipse of the light.

you can try to ignore the past
but you can't ignore
the way it changed you

you are a creature of your scars
like it or not

i think it took me so long to get better
because i got tired
fighting to the top of the mountain
just to fall back to the bottom.

happiness stopped feeling like something
i should fight for.
the best things in life come with a fall,
the mountains come with risks,
love comes with loss,
happiness comes with grief.

regardless we must learn
not to deprive ourselves of the good in life.
we must not stand in the sun
anticipating rainstorms.
life will never be consistent.
the instant we embrace that
we are free.

maybe the only consistency we need to embrace
is the surety of change.
i've decided to stop putting my faith in happiness.
rather i choose to believe there is balance
in the way the good and the bad shake hands.
i choose to believe there is hope
in the change i don't understand.

the thunder isn't always turbulent
it is also peaceful

i'm unwrapping my past
like cruel gifts packaged in brown paper
i'm pulling my trauma
out of the boxes i've been carrying it in
i'm setting it all out in front of me
so that i can cry over it one more time
before i set it all on fire

there are some doors in our minds that we keep locked and there are some doors that we build brick walls in front of because locks aren't enough. you are one of those doors that i don't even acknowledge anymore because you're so far hidden behind the cement blocks i stacked hoping to forget. i may have pushed the memory aside, but emotion has a memory of its own. my heart can't unlive losing you or unlock unloving you. even if i no longer make you the object of my pain, the pain finds its way. seeping through the cracks of the walls in my room and threatening to destroy new relationships in my life. so i'm working on renovating. i'm taking sledgehammers to my safety walls and i'm watching my comfort fall. even though it's scary, i'm allowing myself to remember it all.

i'm learning that the location where healing starts
is the place where my peace falls apart.

there are mornings
when i realize that life can be a process of exploring
rather than a process of finding

it can be a wandering without a certain destination
it can be absorbing sunlight without expectation
it can be dancing for no particular reason at all

perhaps my *purpose* was always to be here
not to discover the reason why

i always do my best thinking on airplanes
something about
walking the wire of mortality
something about
hanging from the sky
supported by only the wind
makes my mind insist
that in this moment
i become a philosopher

perhaps we should all spend more time
on the edge of disaster

not every move you make must be monumental
the key to progress is persistence
not in the magnitude of your movement

comfort can be dangerous.
it keeps you trapped,
hidden from change.

what if all you ever wanted
is just outside in the storm
but you are too comfortable
to move?

proceed from a point of simplicity
collect the small things that are good
and with seashells and wildflowers in hand
you can conquer every storm

we tend to use the word failure
as a pronoun far too often.

you are not your mistakes.

perhaps the worst disease that plagued me was the inability
to see past the present.

the sun was always coming back
i just couldn't see it through the night.

sometimes we don't need someone
to bring back the sun
sometimes we just need someone
to sit with us in the rain

i would let you ruin me
and that's the only way
i know how to say
i love you

i spend a lot of time crying on airplanes
and i think that speaks to
my addiction to movement
and my tendency to leave shards of my soul
everywhere i go

we walked through the same disaster
but we did not emerge the same.
i became strong;
you became bitter.
it has never been about what we went through,
but rather what we are made of.

you did not become who you are
without being who you were
~be kind to your past self

after everything,
what i've learned
is that i will never again beg anyone to love me.
i will not beg anyone to stay.
i will not exist for the purpose
of obtaining anyone's attention.
i will stop treating every conversation like a fight
to gain approval for who i am.
it's okay if not everyone likes me.

just because one person is not impressed,
it doesn't deem me unimpressive.
just because one person doesn't see my worth,
it doesn't deem me unworthy.
just because one person doesn't fall in love,
it doesn't deem me unlovable.

i've realized that setting an expectation for other people often
leads to disappointment.
so i'm setting the expectation exclusively for me.
i do not ask twice for love.
i do not allow the people who walked away from me to take
my worth with them.
i exist in the most authentic way i know how
and wait patiently
for the people who want the real me.

the word "powerless"
used to make me feel weak
now my inability to calm the ocean
or capture the wind
doesn't make me feel weak
it makes me feel free

one of the most difficult lessons i've learned
is that not everything that you love
is meant for you.

being in love with someone
and being right for someone
aren't the same thing

the same applies to everything in life
you will fall in and out of love with a million different places,
sunsets, colors, laughs, voices, books, movies, music.

and you will realize
that some loves stay for a lifetime
and some stay for a little while.
some places are your forever home
and some are temporary.
some voices are constant
and some will echo in your heart forever.

both of these are real
both of these are love
and all of it is life.

dear cloudy days,
i never hated you.
i needed you.

i'm in love with the seasons
i'm done fighting the change
i'm buying flowers for the storm clouds
i'm waltzing with the wind
i'm getting lost in the eye of the storm
i'm melting with the snow
and swaying with the trees

i have found
that the most wonderful moments in my life
the most vibrant sunrises
the people whose names
are permanently carved into my story
have all come to me as a surprise.

so often
the things that feel
out of my control
turn into the memories
that i never want to let go

i don't worry about the weather anymore
when it rains, i dance
when the sun shines, i dance
through it all,
i will dance

the beauty of letting go is this
by loosening your grip
on something you were certain was meant to be
you've made room for what actually is

inevitably change will produce grief.

i look back at that person i was and i don't feel like i know her. such a peculiar feeling to be simultaneously connected and disconnected from myself. at times, i miss her as if she isn't a part of me. i wish for her back as if her eyes are not the ones on the other side of my mirror. i watch old videos of her as if they are a funeral composition.

how peculiar it is,
the way growth and grief hold hands.

i asked the stars
"what do i write about
if nothing has destroyed me lately?"

the cosmos replied
"why do you think you must be destroyed
to be worthy of your voice?"

if the mountains crumble,
mend them with your words.

if the sea is unsettled,
speak for her.

to carry another's brokenness
on your tongue
is often far heavier
than carrying your own.

you will always have a story to tell
when speaking for more than yourself.

i took a walk
on a bridge composed of stars
and each footstep
was fueled by flames.

feet on fire,
i finally remembered
how precious it is
to live.

i hope never again
to forget
how rare it is
that the universe
shares itself with me.

surrender
to
change

i lived in a place
where the sun shone all the time
and i cried
because someone needed to bring
the rain
if not the sky

humans are a lot less concerned with the fact
that we are all going to die
and a lot more concerned with
whether or not they are falling in love.

i think i love that about us.

you don't need to micromanage your healing.
the sun rises each day
whether you ask it to or not.
healing isn't ritualistically forcing yourself
to feel something before you are ready.
it isn't a process of checking boxes.
it is simply absorbing the sunlight when it hits you
and not fighting the rain when it comes.
it is embracing the reality that no one is
waiting on you
to fix yourself.

you have been,
and always will be,
whole as you are.

the decision you must make
is whether
to fill the gaps in your life
with hope
or despair.

it is all a balancing act:
being hard and being soft

you must learn to allow yourself to feel things
without allowing your feelings
to rule the way you react.

you must learn to forgive yourself
but hold yourself accountable.

you must know when to give yourself rest
and when it's time to work.

you must learn to love the things about yourself that you
can't change
while reshaping the things that you can.

i think so many of us have it wrong:
being soft doesn't make you breakable
and being hard doesn't make you indestructible
being both makes you balanced.

there is something raw and freeing
about simply reacting to the universe
the way your core whispers it is necessary.
~just be

i'm running recklessly into thunderstorms
i'm yelling at the sky
and letting the clouds catch my anger
i imagine all my rage
is transformed into lightning

if i cannot fight the storms with my madness
i will allow my madness to become the storm

from the day you arrived on this earth
the world around you has taught you
about your capability to heal yourself.

do you remember scraping your knees
on the playground as a child?
walking around with wounds for weeks,
then suddenly they seemed to disappear?
what makes you think anything has changed?

falling to rising
blood to scabs
scabs to scars
your ability to mend yourself
will also help you heal your heart.
~like the playground

it is not simply
awareness of weakness
that cultivates growth.
it is also the desire for change.
it is embracing the uncomfortable.

it doesn't hurt
like it once did
and that is enough
to go on

i need you to know
you are not broken.
this person that you are
right here,
right now,
is just as whole
as the day you took
your first breath on this earth.
just as human
as before your heart
was betrayed.

sometimes grief makes love a lot harder.
sometimes dishonesty
makes trust feel impossible.
you are not wrong for feeling
like you are trying to sail your boat upstream,
but however difficult it may seem,
you are not damaged,
you are not sinking,
you are still here,

i think that
makes you
strong.

i watched the snow fall
and thought to myself
isn't it funny
how the cold
makes everything a blank canvas again?

the devastation of my heart
has made me cold
but it did not leave me empty.
somewhere inside me
it has begun to snow

i am not ruined.
this is a fresh start.

it took me longer than i'd like
to admit that sometimes love is leaving.
sometimes love is watching from a distance
while you grow on your own.
sometimes love is knowing that
your hand will be much better held
by someone else.

i never knew
that it would feel so heavy
to stop holding you.

i never understood that holding you
was pinning your wings to your sides.
though i am without you now
it is remarkable to watch you fly.

it's always been confusing to me
how one day i can float above the clouds
and the next i cannot rise from my bed.
~inconsistent mental energy

i wish i could heal you
but more than that
i wish for you
to find within yourself
the power it takes
to get back on your feet

it's okay to change.
the ones who love you most
will want to relearn you
at every sunrise

consider the rain
and realize
sometimes it is necessary for the sky to fall
for trees to rise

i dropped my favorite mug this morning.
it shattered on the floor.
love doesn't prevent everything from breaking.

when i say i will love you anyway,
i don't mean that i will love you despite your flaws
despite your brokenness,
despite your bruises.
i mean that i will love those parts of you too.

she stood next to the piece of art and all she could say was "this is devastating, well done."

that was the moment she realized that she could be both broken and beautiful. both imperfect and irreplaceable.

to say that something is devastating is not to say that it is not good or not lovable.

you are a work of art.
you are not meant to keep people still and content.

you were meant to make them move.

the objective isn't to fill every empty space

it is to feel the empty space
to acknowledge it
to sing in it
and listen to your voice
echo off the walls

i didn't start writing about the mountains
until they were in my rearview mirror.
sometimes we can't see the beauty
until it is behind us.

you won't make it out
the same way that you went in
but that is how it is supposed to be
~the woods

on the days that you forget
or your eyes betray the truth
listen to this to remember
and to bring *you* back to you:

you are enough
in every sense of the word
you are enough kindness to fill an ocean
you are enough empathy to still those same seas
you are enough love to fill anyone you see
you are even enough of the not-so-great things.

you are just the right amount of sadness
for someone's arms to fit around
just the right amount of anger
of frustration
of quiet and of loud
all of these things
you are just the right amount.

so next time you doubt
who you are meant to be
please just be you
and that is always enough for me.

something that was keeping me stuck
for a long time was that we use the word "purpose" as a
singular noun, as if we only get one, as if purpose is rare and
hiding somewhere out there for us to find.

i think i've been wasting my time because i've been looking for
fulfillment in one elusive thing. i never stopped to wonder if
perhaps my purpose
is every sunrise i will ever watch, everything i will ever love,
every footstep i will ever take. i think it is possible to find our
path when we stop seeking our purpose and start living for all
our purposes.

challenge yourself to be present
you will find
that awareness of life
becomes love for it.

sometimes i am the moon during the day
out of place
purposeless
lost

sometimes i am the moon during the night
radiant
purposeful
sure

you know the brief moment
when you drive through pouring rain
and suddenly go under a bridge
then the rain momentarily stops

you are the bridge for me

i'm not an optimist
maybe a pessimist
with a great appreciation
for sunrises

don't chase what makes you happy
pursue what make you feel alive.
chase the moments that fill you
and wreck you in the same breath.
love the people
that you would fall apart for.
don't chase contentment
that is temporary and always will be
chase experience and growth.

unravel
and rebuild
and fall apart
and change
and love
and break
and cry

but whatever you do
don't place your hope in happiness
place your hope
in life
in growth
in change.

experience it all
the sun
the fog
the storm
the rain.

to be an author is to befriend the entire world in the most unlikely places. it is to allow everyone who reads your work to meet you in the sacred corners of your mind. it is to make a new friend without leaving your room. it is to be simultaneously lonely and never alone.

to be a reader is to befriend the entire world in the most unlikely places. it is to enter the sacred corners of another's mind. it is to make a new friend without leaving your room. it is to be simultaneously lonely and never alone.

acknowledgments

To you, the reader. I am forever amazed and grateful for the support and enthusiasm you show my books. You make my heart feel seen, and I cannot thank you enough for that. You inspire me to continue writing.

To the first editor of this book, my mom. When I initially self-published *Climate*, you spent countless hours reading and rereading these pages. This book has come so far since then, but I will never forget the time you dedicated and the support you provided. Thanks, Mom.

To my editor at Penguin Life, Meg Leder. I am so fortunate to have you in my corner. Your feedback, patience, and encouragement have helped shape this book into something I am proud to share with the world.

To my literary agent, Laura Lee Mattingly, thank you for believing in me. Your expertise and support have been essential in navigating the path to publication.

Thank you to the team at Penguin Life for helping bring this book to life.

ALSO AVAILABLE

Harmony

*i am finally finding a balance,
a great harmony . . .
between who i was
and who i have become*
—from Harmony

Whitney Hanson chronicles the loss of a loved one through the lens of music. Grief and heartache can make the world go silent, but these rests and pauses in the music are part of the composition of life. It is only by moving through the variations that we can find the harmony and grace that come with healing.

life

Ready to find your next great read? Let us help. Visit prh.com/nextread

Home

*but if you can find a home within yourself
and make peace with your bees
you will be alright
—from* Home

Resonant, raw, and vibrant, *Home* is a lyrical map to navigating heartbreak. Tracing the stages of healing, from the despair that comes with the end of a relationship to the eventual light and liberation that come with time, the poems in *Home* provide comfort and solace, while revitalizing your soul—and helping you make peace with your bees.

life

01 14